Irish Kids Songs & Rhymes

Plus Many Beloved Traditional Songs

A Mama Lisa Book

Irish Kids Songs & Rhymes
Plus Many Beloved Traditional Songs
A Mama Lisa Book

Original Material Written by Lisa Yannucci

Translations by Monique Palomares and Lisa Yannucci

Additional Translations by Our Many Correspondents

Compiled and Edited by Jason Pomerantz

Visit Mama Lisa on the web at **www.MamaLisa.com**

Contents

Introduction

Songs & Rhymes

30. It's a Long Way to Tipperary

31. Janey Mac

32. Lámh, lámh eile (Hand, Other Hand)

33. Little Jennie Whiteface

34. May the Road Rise to Meet You

35. Me Mother Is Gone to Church

36. Michael Finnigan

37. Mitty Matty Had a Hen

38. Oíche Shamhna (Halloween, Halloween)

39. Old Dan Tucker

40. Old Mother Witch

41. Old Riley's Daughter

42. One Potato, Two Potato

43. Onery, Twoery, Dickery, Davey

44. One, Two, Three O'Leary

45. Paddy on the Railway

Thanks and Acknowledgements

About Us

Introduction

Ireland! Emerald green isle... land of shamrocks, fairies and leprechauns. Home of St. Patrick, Yeats and James Joyce... Rolling green hills and, of course, potatoes!

In this book we've gathered over 60 Irish children's songs and rhymes. Many have commentary sent to us by our correspondents who are immersed in the traditions and culture of Ireland.

There's not always a sharp distinction between songs sung by children and by adults. So we've included a sampling of some of the most popular Irish traditional songs. We've also included examples of Ireland's heritage of very moving ballads and lullabies.

Many of these songs and rhymes are in English, but we're proud to also include several that are Gaelic. In those cases we provide English translations.

I'm proud to say I have some Irish blood myself - my great grandmother who I still remember from when I was a wee one.... I always think of her on St. Patrick's day when my family makes corn beef and cabbage with Irish soda bread and we drink a Guinness or a Black and Tan.... I feel particularly proud to wear green on that day!

At Mama Lisa's World we work with ordinary people around the globe to build a platform to preserve and exchange traditional culture. Most of the songs and rhymes featured here have been provided by our contributors, to whom we're very grateful! (Please see the Thanks and Acknowledgements section for a complete list of everyone who has contributed.) We love to receive new (public domain) material, so if one of your favorites has not been included, please visit our website and write us to let us know.

The material presented here is part of a living tradition. So the version of a song you know may have some different words. Tell us about it! We consider our collection a dialogue and we update it all the time with your comments.

At the end of each item in this book, there's a web address to an online version of the song or rhyme. There we are often able to include sheet music, recordings and videos of performances.

We hope this book will help foster a love of Irish songs and culture all over the world!

"MAY YOUR POCKETS BE HEAVY AND YOUR HEART BE LIGHT, MAY GOOD LUCK PURSUE YOU EACH MORNING AND NIGHT."

Slán anois!

Mama Lisa
(Lisa Yannucci)
www.mamalisa.com

Kid Songs and Rhymes

Including Traditional Songs

1, 2, 3, Me Mother Caught a Flea

1, 2, 3, Me Mother Caught a Flea
(Nursery Rhyme)

One, two, three,
Me mother caught a flea,
She put it in the teapot
And made a cup of tea.
The flea jumped out,
Me mother gave a shout
And in came daddy
With his shirt hanging out.

Photos & Illustrations

For more about 1, 2, 3, Me Mother Caught a Flea, go to:
http://www.mamalisa.com/?t=es&p=3508.

There, you'll find a video performance.

Adam and Eve and Pinch Me
(Nursery Rhyme Game)

1ST CHILD SAYS:

"Adam and Eve and Pinch Me
Went down to the river to bathe;
Adam and Eve were drowned,
Who do you think was saved?"

2ND CHILD REPLIES:

"Pinch Me"

THEN THE 1ST CHILD PINCHES THE 2ND ONE.

Notes

Alternate 2nd line: "WENT DOWN TO THE RIVER TO PLAY".

For more about Adam and Eve and Pinch Me, go to:
http://www.mamalisa.com/?t=es&p=3465.

A haon, a dó, muc is bó (One, Two, A Pig and A Cow)

A haon, a dó, muc is bó
(Irish Gaelic Nursery Rhyme)

A haon, a dó, muc is bó,
A trí, a ceathair, bróga leathair,
A cúig, a sé, cupán tae,
A seacht, a hocht, seanbhean bhocht,
A naoi, a deich, císte te.

One, Two, A Pig and A Cow
(English Translation)

One, two, a pig and a cow,
Three, four, leather shoes,
Five, six, a cup of tea,
Seven, eight, a poor old lady,
Nine, ten, a hot cake.

For more about A haon, a dó, muc is bó , go to:
http://www.mamalisa.com/?t=es&p=3471.

Are You a Witch or Are You a Fairy?

This jump rope rhyme is about Bridget Cleary, an Irish woman who was killed by her husband in 1895. Her husband Michael Cleary said he killed her because he believed she was abducted by fairies and replaced by a changeling.

Are You a Witch or Are You a Fairy?

(Jump Rope Chant)

Are you a witch or
Are you a fairy?
Or are you the wife
of Michael Cleary?

Notes

What's odd about this case is that about nine of the couple's family and friends were present at the time of Bridget Cleary's death. He had convinced them that she was a changeling or witch. Michael put his wife on fire and kept the people present from doing anything to help her. But it seems they were there in the first place to help him rid his wife of evil forces. They all went to trial and Michael was imprisoned. Bridget's death is referred to as the last witch burning in Ireland.

For more about Are You a Witch or Are You a Fairy?, go to:
http://www.mamalisa.com/?t=es&p=3466.

As I Went up the Apple Tree

As I Went up the Apple Tree
(Nursery Rhyme)

As I went up the apple tree
All the apples fell on me.
Apple pudding, apple pie
Did you ever tell a lie?

For more about As I Went up the Apple Tree, go to:
http://www.mamalisa.com/?t=es&p=3513.

6

Ballyeamon Cradle Song
(Lullaby)

Rest tired eyes a while
Sweet is thy baby's smile,
Angels are guarding
And they watch o'er thee.

Sleep, sleep, grah mo chree*
Here on your mamma's knee,
Angels are guarding
And they watch o'er thee,

The birdeens sing a fluting song
They sing to thee the whole day long,
Wee fairies dance o'er hill and the dale
For very love of thee.

Notes

*GRAH MO CHREE *means my love, my darling or my sweetheart in Irish Gaelic. It's the Anglicized form of the Gaelic "grá mo chroí" that literally means "love of my heart".*

For more about Ballyeamon Cradle Song, go to:
http://www.mamalisa.com/?t=es&p=3498.

There, you'll find a video performance.

Bog Down in The Valley-O

Bog Down in The Valley-O
(Traditional Song)

(Chorus)
O-ro the rattlin' bog,
The bog down in the valley-o
O-ro the rattlin' bog,
The bog down in the valley-o

And in that bog there was a tree,
A rare tree, a rattlin' tree
With the tree in the bog
And the bog down in the valley-o.

(Chorus)

Now on that tree there was a limb,
A rare limb, a rattlin' limb
With the limb on the tree
And the tree in the bog
And the bog down in the valley-o.

(Chorus)

Now on that limb there was a branch,
A rare branch, a rattlin' branch
With the branch on the limb

And the limb on the tree
And the tree in the bog
And the bog down in the valley-o.

(Chorus)

Now on that branch there was a twig,
A rare twig, a rattlin' twig
With the twig on the branch,
And the branch on the limb
And the limb on the tree
And the tree in the bog
And the bog down in the valley-o.

(Chorus)

Now on that twig there was a nest,
A rare nest, a rattlin' nest
With the nest on the twig,
And the twig on the branch,
And the branch on the limb
And the limb on the tree
And the tree in the bog
And the bog down in the valley-o.

(Chorus)

Now in that nest there was an egg,
A rare egg, a rattlin' egg,
With the egg in the nest,
And the nest on the twig,
And the twig on the branch,
And the branch on the limb
And the limb on the tree
And the tree in the bog
And the bog down in the valley-o.

(Chorus)

Now in that egg there was a bird,
A rare bird, a rattlin' bird
With the bird in the egg,
And the egg in the nest,
And the nest on the twig,
And the twig on the branch,
And the branch on the limb
And the limb on the tree
And the tree in the bog
And the bog down in the valley-o.

(Chorus)

Now on that bird there was a feather,
A rare feather, a rattlin' feather,

With the feather on the bird,
And the bird in the egg,
And the egg in the nest,
And the nest on the twig,
And the twig on the branch,
And the branch on the limb
And the limb on the tree
And the tree in the bog
And the bog down in the valley-o.

(Chorus)

Now on that feather there was a flea,
A rare flea, a rattlin' flea
With the flea on the feather,
And the feather on the bird,
And the bird in the egg,
And the egg in the nest,
And the nest on the twig,
And the twig on the branch,
And the branch on the limb
And the limb on the tree
And the tree in the bog
And the bog down in the valley-o.

(Chorus)

For more about Bog Down in The Valley-O, go to:
http://www.mamalisa.com/?t=es&p=3013.

There, you'll find sheet music, a MIDI melody and a video performance.

Bold O'Donahue
(Traditional Song)

Well, here I am from Paddy's land, a land of high renown
I've broke the hearts of all the girls for miles round Keady town
And when they hear that I'm awa' they'll raise a hullabaloo
When they hear about that handsome lad they call O'Donahue!

(Chorus)
For I'm the boy to please her, and I'm the boy to tease her
I'm the boy to squeeze her, an' I'll tell you what I'll do
I'll court her like an Irishman, wi' me brogue and blarney too is me plan
With the holligan, rolligan, swolligan, molligan bold O`Donahue!*

I wish me love was a red, red rose growing on yon garden wall
And me to be a dewdrop and upon her brow I'd fall!
Perhaps now she might think of me as a rather heavy dew
And no more she'd love that handsome lad they call O'Donahue!

(Chorus)

I hear that Queen Victoria has a daughter fine and grand
Perhaps she'd take it into her head for to marry an Irishman
And if I could only get the chance to have a word or two
I'm sure she'd take a notion to the bold O'Donahue!

(Chorus)

Notes

*Alternate version of this line: "With the rollikin swollikin hollikin wollikin bold
O'Donahue!"*

For more about Bold O'Donahue, go to:
http://www.mamalisa.com/?t=es&p=3468.

There, you'll find a video performance.

Briney Ole Lynn

*This song is a variation of **Bryan O'Lynn**.*

Briney Ole Lynn
(Traditional Song)

Briney Ole Lynn had no britches to wear
He stole him a sheep skin to make him a pair
The wooly side out and the skinny side in*.
"A mighty fine pair," said Briney Ole Lynn.

Tra La La La La La La La La La La La thru the whole tune.

Have you ever been into a bachelor's shanty
Where water is scarce and whiskey is plenty?
A three legged table and a chair to match
The door on the shanty ain't got any latch.

Tra La La La La La La thru the whole tune again.

Notes

Marcy wrote: "Could have been skinny side out and the wooly side in."

For more about Briney Ole Lynn, go to:
http://www.mamalisa.com/?t=es&p=2687.

There, you'll find a video performance.

Bryan O'Lynn

*This song is a variation of **Briney Ole Lynn**.*

Bryan O'Lynn
(Traditional Song)

Bryan O'Lynn was a gentleman born,
He lived at a time when no clothes they were worn,
But as fashion went out, of course Bryan walked in,
"Whoo! I'll soon lead the fashions," says Bryan O'Lynn.

Bryan O'Lynn had no breeches to wear
He got a sheepskin for to make him a pair,
With the fleshy side out, and the woolly side in,
"Whoo! They're pleasant and cool," says Bryan O'Lynn.

Bryan O'Lynn had no shirt to his back,
He went to a neighbor's and borrowed a sack,
Then he puckered the meal bag up under his chin,
"Whoo! They'll take them for ruffles," says Bryan O'Lynn.

Bryan O'Lynn had no hat to his head,
He thought that the pot would do him instead,
Then he murdered a cod for the sake of its fin,
"Whoo! 'twill pass for a feather," says Bryan O'Lynn.

Bryan O'Lynn was hard up for a coat,
He borrowed a skin of a neighboring goat,
With the horns sticking out from his oxters, and then,
"Whoo! They'll take them for pistols," says Bryan O'Lynn.

Bryan O'Lynn had no stockings to wear,
He bought a rat's skin to make him a pair,
He then drew them over his manly shin,
"Whoo! They're illegant wear," says Bryan O'Lynn.

Bryan O'Lynn had no brogues to his toes,
He hopped on two crab shells to serve him for those,
Then he split up two oysters that matched just like twins,
"Whoo! They'll shine out like buckles," says Bryan O'Lynn.

Bryan O'Lynn had no watch to put on,
He scooped out a turnip to make him a one,
Then he planted a cricket in under the skin -
"Whoo! They'll think it's a-ticking," says Bryan O'Lynn.

Bryan O'Lynn to his house had no door,
He'd the sky for a roof and the bog for a floor,
He'd a way to jump out, and a way to swim in,
"Whoo! It's very convaynient," says Bryan O'Lynn.

Bryan O'Lynn, his wife, and wife's mother,
They all went home o'er the bridge together,
The bridge it broke down and they all tumbled in,
"Whoo! We'll go home by water," says Bryan O'Lynn.

Notes

*Bryan O'Lynn seems to come from the song Tom O'Lin. Tom O'lin is also known as "Thom of Lyn" and before that "Tamlene" or "Tam Lin". The oldest reference to Tom O'Lin is in "**The complaynt of Scotland: Written in 1548** (http://books.google.com/books?id=A2QaAAAAYAAJ&printsec=frontcover&dq= Complaynt+of+Scotland&cd=1#v=onepage&q=lyn&f=false)".*

***Tom a lyn from the ballad** (http://www.tam-lin.org/front.html) is Tom Thumb (originally a dwarf from Scandinavia called Thaumlin). (Ref. "**An explanatory and pronouncing dictionary of the noted names of fiction** (http://books.google.com/books?id=kMQNAAAAYAAJ&pg=PA364&dq=tom+of+ lyn&cd=9#v=onepage&q=tom%20of%20lyn&f=false) (1893). He is also called Tommelfinger (thumb) in Danish and Brian O'Lynn in Ireland.*

There are several versions of these Tom O'Lin songs.

Comments

*You can **see and hear yet another version** (http://www.chivalry.com/cantaria/lyrics/brian_olynn.html) online.*

For more about Bryan O'Lynn, go to: **http://www.mamalisa.com/?t=es&p=2686**.

There, you'll find a video performance.

Cockles and Mussels

This song is also called MOLLY MALONE.

Cockles and Mussels
(Folk Song)

In Dublin's fair city,
Where the girls are so pretty,
I first set my eyes on sweet Molly Malone,
As she wheel'd her wheel barrow,
Thro' streets broad and narrow...

(Chorus)
Crying, "Cockles and Mussels alive, alive-O!
Alive, alive-O! Alive, alive-O!"
Crying, "Cockles and Mussels alive, alive-O!"

She was a fishmonger,
But sure 'twas no wonder,
For so were her father and mother before,
And they each wheel'd their barrow

Thro' streets broad and narrow...

(Repeat Chorus)

She died of a fever,
And no one could save her,
And that was the end of sweet Molly Malone.
But her ghost wheels her barrow
Thro' streets broad and narrow...

(Repeat Chorus)

Notes

This song was written and composed by James Yorkston (who was Scottish).

*****

Cockles and Mussels - Margaret's Version
(Also called MOLLY MALONE*)*

In Dublin's fair city,
Where the girls are so pretty,
There lived a fishmonger,
Named Molly Malone,
And she wheeled her wheelbarrow,
Through the streets broad and narrow...

(Chorus)
Crying, "Cockles and Mussels alive, alive-O!
Alive, alive-O! Alive, alive-O!"
Crying, "Cockles and Mussels alive, alive-O!"

She was a fishmonger,
A fishmonger's daughter.
Her father's grandfathers
Were fishmongers too.
And they wheeled their wheelbarrows
Through the streets broad and narrow...

(Repeat Chorus)
Crying, "Cockles and Mussels alive, alive-O!
Alive, alive-O! Alive, alive-O!"
Crying, "Cockles and Mussels alive, alive-O!"

She died of the fever,
T'was nothing could save her,
And that was the end of
Sweet Molly Malone.
Now her ghost wheels her barrow
Through streets broad and narrow...

(Repeat Chorus)
Crying, "Cockles and Mussels alive, alive-O!
Alive, alive-O! Alive, alive-O!"
Crying, "Cockles and Mussels alive, alive-O!"

Photos & Illustrations

For more about Cockles and Mussels, go to:
http://www.mamalisa.com/?t=es&p=419.

There, you'll find sheet music, a MIDI melody and a video performance.

Colcannon

Colcannon is a common Irish dish that's traditionally made with kale or cabbage, mashed potatoes, scallions, butter, milk, Irish bacon, salt and pepper.

It's long been a tradition to eat Colcannon on Halloween. For this holiday, symbolic items are hidden in the Colcannon: a coin, a thimble, a button and a plain gold ring. Whoever gets the coin will be rich. The person who gets the thimble or button will remain unmarried, and the one who gets the golden ring will get married within the year.

Colcannon
(Halloween Song)

Did you ever eat Colcannon, made from lovely pickled cream?
With the greens and scallions mingled like a picture in a dream.
Did you ever make a hole on top to hold the melting flake
Of the creamy, flavoured butter that your mother used to make?

(Chorus)

Oh you did, so you did, so did he and so did I.
And the more I think about it, sure, the nearer I'm to cry.
Oh, weren't them the happy days when troubles we had not,
And our mothers made Colcannon in the little skillet pot.

Well did you ever take potato cake in a basket to the school,
Tucked underneath your oxter (1) with your book, your slate and rule?
And when teacher wasn't looking, sure, a great big bite you'd take,
Of the creamy flavoured butter and sweet potato cake.

(Chorus)

Well did you ever go a-courting as the evening sun went down,
And the moon began a-peeping from behind the Hill o' Down?
As you wandered down the boreen (2) where the clúrachán (3) was seen,
And you whispered loving phrases to your little fair Colleen.

(Chorus)

Notes

(1) Armpit
(2) Little road
(3) Leprechaun

For more about Colcannon, go to: **http://www.mamalisa.com/?t=es&p=3504**.

There, you'll find a video performance.

Connemara Cradle Song

Connemara is an area in the west of Ireland that borders on the Atlantic Ocean. It includes the Bay at Barna and Killary Harbour.

Connemara Cradle Song
(Lullaby)

On the wings of the wind o'er the dark rolling deep
Angels are coming to watch o'er thy sleep
Angels are coming to watch over thee
So list to the wind coming over the sea.

(Chorus)
Hear the wind blow love, hear the wind blow
Lean your head over and hear the wind blow
Hear the wind blow love, hear the wind blow
Hang your head over and hear the wind blow.

Oh, winds of the night, may your fury be crossed
May no one who's dear to our island be lost
Blow the winds gently, calm be the foam
Shine the light brightly and guide them back home.

(Chorus)

The currachs* are sailing way out on the blue
Laden with herring of silvery hue
Silver the herring and silver the sea
And soon there'll be silver for baby and me.

(Chorus)

The currachs tomorrow will stand on the shore
And daddy goes sailing, sailing no more
The nets will be drying, the nets heaven blessed
And safe in my arms dear, contented he'll rest.

(Chorus)

Notes

A currach is a wooden Irish row boat. In the old days, skins were stretched over its wooden frame.

Photos & Illustrations

Comments

*Monique wrote, "It's the same tune -or a slight variant- of '**Down in the valley, valley so low, hang your head over hear the wind blow** (http://www.mamalisa.com/?t=es&p=2286&c=23)' as sung by Pete Seeger".*

For more about Connemara Cradle Song , go to:
http://www.mamalisa.com/?t=es&p=3499.

There, you'll find a video performance.

14

Dan, Dan, The Fine Old Man
(Nursery Rhyme)

Dan, Dan, the fine old man,
Washed his face in the frying pan,
Combed his hair with the leg of the chair,
Dan, Dan, the fine old man.

For more about Dan, Dan, The Fine Old Man , go to:
http://www.mamalisa.com/?t=es&p=3529.

Danny Boy

DANNY BOY is an important song for Irish Americans and Irish Canadians. It's sung on St. Patrick's Day and sometimes at funerals.

Danny Boy
(Traditional Song)

Oh, Danny boy, the pipes, the pipes are calling
From glen to glen, and down the mountain side
The summer's gone, and all the flowers are dying
'Tis you, 'tis you must go and I must bide.

But come ye back when summer's in the meadow
Or when the valley's hushed and white with snow
'Tis I'll be here in sunshine or in shadow
Oh, Danny boy, oh, Danny boy, I love you so.

And when you come, and all the flowers are dying
If I am dead, as dead I well may be
You'll come and find the place where I am lying
And kneel and say an "Ave" there for me.

And I shall hear, though soft you tread above me
And all my grave shall warm and sweeter be
For you will bend and tell me that you love me
And I shall sleep in peace until you come to me.

Notes

Written by Englishman Frederic Weatherly and set to the tune of "Londonderry Air".

There are slightly different versions of DANNY BOY.

For more about Danny Boy, go to: **http://www.mamalisa.com/?t=es&p=3506**.

There, you'll find sheet music, a MIDI melody and a video performance.

16

Dilín ó deamhas (Forever Oh)

This is a song to sing with a little kid in your lap. The chorus seems to be nonsense and most people don't even try to translate it. I was able to find some meaning of the words by searching back in old Irish Gaelic dictionaries. Here's what I came up with...

Dilín ó deamhas
(Irish Gaelic Children's Lap Game Song)

(Curfá)
Dilín ó deamhas ó deamhas
Dilín ó deamhas ó dí
Dilín ó deamhas ó deamhas ó deamhas ó
Dilín ó deamhas ó dí

Chuiread* mo rún chun suain,
Chuiread mo rún 'na luí,
Chuiread mo rún chun suain go ciúin,
Le dilín ó deamhas ó dí.

(Curfá)

Is buachaill aniar aniar,
Is buachaill aniar an fear,
Is buachaill aniar aniar aniar,
'S is cailín ón sliabh a bhean.

(Curfá)

Caithimis suas is suas é,
Caithimis suas an páiste,
Caithimis suas is suas is suas é,
'S tiocfaidh sé 'nuas amárach.

(Curfá)

Forever Oh
(English Translation)

(Chorus)
Forever oh shears oh shears
Forever oh shears oh need
Forever oh shears oh shears oh shears oh
Forever oh shears oh need.

I lulled my darling to sleep
I put my darling to bed
I lulled my darling to sleep to sleep,
For forever oh shears, oh need.

(Chorus)

The boy is from the West, the West,
The boy is from the West, a man,
The boy is from the West, West, West,
And the girl from the mountain his lady.

(Chorus)

Throw him upwards and up,
Throw the child up,
Throw him upwards and up and up,
And he will come down tomorrow.

Notes

Definitions for words in the chorus:

Deamhas = shears or sheep-shears
Dilín = never, ever, forever
ó = from, since, oh
di = little or want/need (?)

*Can anyone confirm the meaning of the words in the chorus? Please **email me** if you can. Thanks! Lisa*

Comments

*You can listen to this song **here** (http://www.askaboutireland.ie/aai-files/assets/ebooks/talking%20ebooks/songs/Dilin%282%29.swf).*

For more about Dilín ó deamhas, go to:
http://www.mamalisa.com/?t=es&p=3462.

There, you'll find a video performance.

Do You Love an Apple?

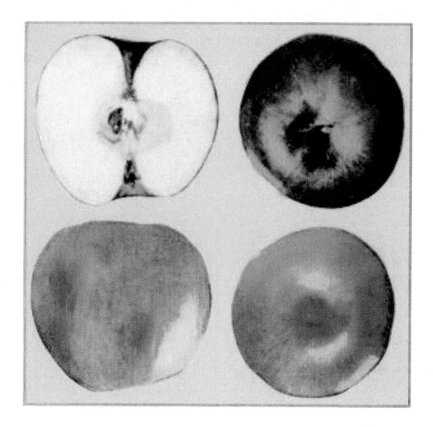

There are different versions of this song.

Do You Love an Apple?
(Folk Song)

Do you love an apple,
Do you love a pear?
Do you love a laddie
with curly brown hair?

(Chorus)
Oh but still, I love him,
I can't deny him,
I will go with him

Wherever he goes.

Before I got married
I wore a black shawl,
But now that I'm married
I wear bugger-all.

(Chorus)

He stood at the corner,
A fag in his mouth
Two hands in his pockets,
He whistled me out.

(Chorus)

He works at the pier
For nine pounds a week,
On Saturday night
He comes rolling home drunk.

(Chorus)

Before I got married
I'd sport and I'd play,
But now the cradle
It gets in me way.

(Chorus)

Do you love an apple,
Do you love a pear?
Do you love a laddie
with curly brown hair?

(Chorus)

For more about Do You Love an Apple?, go to:
http://www.mamalisa.com/?t=es&p=3503.

There, you'll find a video performance.

18

Fairy Lullaby

"The strange and weird superstition, concerning the carrying off by the fairies of
children, is well known... But the fairies carried off adults also, as the following
song will show.... It is necessary to observe that the person who speaks is the one
who has been carried off by the fairies, and set with others who had undergone the
same fate to nurse the stolen babies. If not delivered, within a year and a day, she
was to be made queen of the fairy fort, and would henceforth be lost to mortal ken.
She perceives a woman washing on the brink of a stream, and informs her of these
facts, and of the manner in which she may be liberated, whilst still hushing the

baby to sleep. There is much pathos in her allusion to the fact that she is nursing a strange babe, whilst her own remains without a mother's care. " -The Shamrock (1870)

Fairy Lullaby
(Lullaby)

O woman, washing beside the river,
Hush-a-by baby, babe not mine,
My woeful wail, do you pity never?
Hush-a-by baby, babe not mine,
A year ago I was snatched for ever,
Hush-a-by baby, babe not mine,
From my home to the hill where hawthorns quiver,
Hush-a-by baby, babe not mine,
Shoheen sho, ulolo,
Shoheen sho, strange baby O!
Shoheen sho, ulolo,
You're not my own sweet baby O!

'Tis there the fairy-court is holden,
Hush-a-by baby, babe not mine,
And there flow beor and ale so olden,
Hush-a-by baby, babe not mine,
And there are combs of honey golden,
Hush-a-by baby, babe not mine,
And there lie men in bonds enfolden,
Hush-a-by baby, babe not mine.
Shoheen sho, ulolo,
Shoheen sho, strange baby O!
Shoheen sho, ulolo,
You're not my own sweet baby O!

How many are there of fairest faces,
Hush-a-by baby, babe not mine,
Bright-eyed boys with manly graces,
Hush-a-by baby, babe not mine.
Gold-haired girls with curling tresses,
Hush-a-by baby, babe not mine,
And mothers who nurse - with sad caresses,
Hush-a-by baby, babe not mine,
Shoheen sho, ulolo,
Shoheen sho, strange baby O!
Shoheen sho, ulolo,
You're not my own sweet baby O!

O, tell my husband to come to-morrow,
Hush-a-by baby, babe not mine,
A waxen taper he first shall borrow,
Hush-a-by baby, babe not mine,
And black knife bring to cross my sorrow,
Hush-a-by baby, babe not mine,

And stab the flank of the first steed thorough,
Hush-a-by baby, babe not mine,
Shoheen sho, ulolo,
Shoheen sho, strange baby O!
Shoheen sho, ulolo,
You're not my own sweet baby O!

Say, pluck the herb where hawthorns quiver,
Hush-a-by baby, babe not mine,
And wish a wish that God may deliver,
Hush-a-by baby, babe not mine,
If he come not now - he need come never,
Hush-a-by baby, babe not mine,
For I shall be Queen of these Fairies for ever,
Hush-a-by baby, babe not mine.
Shoheen sho, ulolo,
Shoheen sho, strange baby O!
Shoheen sho, ulolo,
You're not my own sweet baby O!

Notes

"The lullaby line addressed to the baby is to be read in a lower tone than the rest, being marked piano in the music. This line differs in different Irish copies, so that, in place of 'Hush-a-by baby, babe not mine,' the reader might say simply: 'Shoheen sho, strange baby O!' or, 'Sho hoo lo, sho hoo lo.'" -The Shamrock (1870)

For more about Fairy Lullaby, go to: **http://www.mamalisa.com/?t=es&p=3500**.

Four Ducks on a Pond

This poem was written by Irishman William Allingham (1824 - 1889).

Four Ducks on a Pond
(Nursery Rhyme)

Four ducks on a pond,
A grass bank beyond,
A blue sky of spring,
White clouds on the wing:
What a little thing
To remember for years,
To remember with tears!

For more about Four Ducks on a Pond, go to:
http://www.mamalisa.com/?t=es&p=3459.

Frosty Weather

Frosty Weather
(Nursery Rhyme)

Frosty weather,
Snowy weather,
When the wind blows
We all go together.

For more about Frosty Weather, go to:
http://www.mamalisa.com/?t=es&p=3512.

Goodie on a Saucer

Goodie on a Saucer
(Children's Song)

We know what Bill Binkie* wants
We know what Bill Binkie wants
We know what Bill Binkie wants
It's a goodie on a saucer.

We know what is good for him
We know what is good for him
We know what is good for him
It's a goodie on a saucer.

Notes

Put in a person's first and last names.

For more about Goodie on a Saucer, go to:
http://www.mamalisa.com/?t=es&p=3525.

There, you'll find a video performance.

Head of Hair Forehead Bare

"This is the version I learned from my nana here in Ireland..." -Caroline

Head of Hair Forehead Bare
(Nursery Rhyme)

Head of hair
Forehead bare
Eye winker
Tommy tinker
Nose dropper
Mouth eater
Chin chopper chin chin.

Notes

This fun game helps teach little kids the names of different parts of the face.

Game Instructions

Point to the part of the face mentioned as you say the line.

Comments

Check out MAMA LISA'S WORLD BLOG *to read more versions of **rhymes about names for the parts of the face** (http://www.mamalisa.com/blog/do-you-know-one-that-starts-head-knocker-eye-blinker/).*

For more about Head of Hair Forehead Bare, go to:
http://www.mamalisa.com/?t=es&p=3432.

23

Hiddledy, Diddledy, Dumpty
(Nursery Rhyme)

Hiddledy, diddledy, dumpty,
The cat ran up the plum tree;
Half-a-crown to fetch her down,
Hiddledy, diddledy, dumpty.

For more about Hiddledy, Diddledy, Dumpty, go to:
http://www.mamalisa.com/?t=es&p=3514.

How Many Miles to Dublin?

Here's a nice little Irish nursery rhyme…

How Many Miles to Dublin?
(Nursery Rhyme)

How many miles to Dub-l-in?
Three score* and ten,
Will we be there by candle-light?
Yes and back again;
Hupp, hupp my little horse,
Hupp, hupp, again.

Notes

*Three score is sixty.

For more about How Many Miles to Dublin?, go to:
http://www.mamalisa.com/?t=es&p=1755.

I am the Wee Falorie Man

I am the Wee Falorie Man
(Children's Song)

I am the wee falorie man
A rattling, roving Irishman,
I can do all that ever you can
For I am the wee falorie man.

I have a sister Mary Ann
She washes her face in the frying pan,
And out she goes to hunt for a man
I have a sister Mary Ann.

I am a good old working man,

Each day I carry a wee tin can
A large penny bap* and a clipe** of ham
I am a good old working man.

Notes

*A "penny bap" is a flattish round bun
**A "clipe" is a little chunk

Comments

It's common to only sing the first verse of this song.

For more about I am the Wee Falorie Man, go to:
http://www.mamalisa.com/?t=es&p=3461.

There, you'll find a video performance.

I Know Where I'm Going
(Folk Song)

I know where I'm going
And I know who's going with me
I know who I love
And the dear knows who I'll marry.

I have stockings of silk
And shoes of bright green leather
Combs to buckle my hair
And a ring for every finger.

Some say he's black*
But I say he's bonnie
The fairest of them all
My handsome winsome Johnny.

Feather beds are soft
And painted rooms are bonny
But I would leave them all
To go with my love my Johnny.

I know where I'm going
And I know who's going with me
I know who I love
But the dear knows who I'll marry.

Notes

We believe this is referring to his hair color.

For more about I Know Where I'm Going, go to:
http://www.mamalisa.com/?t=es&p=3502.

There, you'll find a video performance.

I'm a Tiny Tiny Thing

I couldn't resist including this rhyme in our collection. It has such a wonderful ring to it! It comes from James Joyce's ULYSSES *and is from the point of view of a moth.*

I'm a Tiny Tiny Thing
(Nursery Rhyme)

I'm a tiny tiny thing
Ever flying in the spring
Round and round a ringaring.
Long ago I was a king
Now I do this kind of thing
On the wing, on the wing!
Bing!
Pretty pretty pretty pretty
Pretty pretty petticoats.

For more about I'm a Tiny Tiny Thing, go to:
http://www.mamalisa.com/?t=es&p=1468.

Irish Lullaby (Sho-heen)
(Lullaby)

I'd rock my own sweet childie* to rest
In a cradle of gold on a bough of the willow,
To the shosheen** ho of the wind of the west
And the shularoo of the soft sea billow.
Sleep, baby dear,
Sleep without fear,
Mother is here beside your pillow.

I'd put my own sweet childie to sleep
In a silver boat on the beautiful river,
Where a shosheen whisper the white cascades,
And a shularoo the green flags shiver.
Sleep, baby dear,
Sleep without fear,
Mother is here with you forever.

Shularoo! to the rise and fall of mother's bosom
'tis sleep has bound you,
And O, my child, what cozier nest for rosier rest
could love have found you?
Sleep, baby dear,
Sleep without fear,
Mother's two arms are clasped around you.

Notes

"Childie" means "child".
**Sometimes "shosheen" is "sho-heen" and the "shularoo" in the next line is "sho hoo lo". If you sing it the 2nd way you should substitute these words in all the verses.*

Comments

This lullaby was written by Alfred Perceval Graves (1846-1931) and published in his book "Songs of Killarney" in 1873.

For more about Irish Lullaby (Sho-heen), go to:
http://www.mamalisa.com/?t=es&p=3538.

There, you'll find a video performance.

I See the Moon, The Moon Sees Me

"On the first appearance of the new moon, a number of children linked hands and danced, keeping time to the following verse..." -P.W. Joyce

I See the Moon, The Moon Sees Me
(Nursery Rhyme)

I see the moon, the moon sees me,
God bless the moon and God bless me:
There's grace in the cottage and grace in the hall;
And the grace of God is over us all.

For more about I See the Moon, The Moon Sees Me, go to:
http://www.mamalisa.com/?t=es&p=3469.

There, you'll find a MIDI melody.

It's a Long Way to Tipperary

People often sing only the chorus to this song. The full version starts with the first verse and then goes into the chorus.

It's a Long Way to Tipperary
(Traditional Song)

(Chorus)
It's a long way to Tipperary,
It's a long way to go.
It's a long way to Tipperary
To the sweetest girl I know!
Goodbye, Piccadilly,
Farewell, Leicester Square!
It's a long long way to Tipperary,
But my heart's right there.

Up to mighty London
Came an Irishman one day.
As the streets are paved with gold
Sure, everyone was gay,
Singing songs of Piccadilly,
Strand and Leicester Square,
Till Paddy got excited,
Then he shouted to them there:

(Chorus)

Paddy wrote a letter
To his Irish Molly-O,
Saying, "Should you not receive it,
Write and let me know!
If I make mistakes in spelling,
Molly, dear," said he,
"Remember, it's the pen that's bad,

Don't lay the blame on me!"

(Chorus)

Molly wrote a neat reply
To Irish Paddy-O,
Saying Mike Maloney
Wants to marry me, and so
Leave the Strand and Piccadilly
Or you'll be to blame,
For love has fairly drove me silly:
Hoping you're the same!

(Chorus)

Notes

Written by Jack Judge in 1912. Judge was born in England in 1872. His parents were Irish, and his grandparents were from Tipperary, Ireland.

For more about It's a Long Way to Tipperary , go to:
http://www.mamalisa.com/?t=es&p=3437.

There, you'll find a video performance.

Janey Mac

"Janey Mac" is an expression of surprise. It's also spelled "Janey Mack".

Janey Mac
(Nursery Rhyme)

Janey Mac me shirt is black,
What'll I do for Sunday?
Go to bed and cover your head,
And don't get up till Monday.

For more about Janey Mac, go to: **http://www.mamalisa.com/?t=es&p=3527**.

Lámh, lámh eile (Hand, Other Hand)

*This is the Gaelic equivalent of **Head, Shoulders, Knees and Toes** (http://www.mamalisa.com/?t=es&p=680&c=23)....*

Lámh, lámh eile
(Irish Gaelic Nursery Rhyme)

Lámh, lámh eile, a haon, a dó,
Cos, cos eile, a haon, a dó.
Ceann, srón, béil, smig,
Agus fiacla bána i mo bhéal istigh.
Súil, súil eile, a haon, a dó,
Cluas, cluas eile, a haon, a dó,
Ceann, srón, béil, smig,
Agus fiacla bána i mo bhéal istigh.

Hand, Other Hand
(English Translation)

Hand, other hand, one, two,
Leg, other leg, one, two,
Head, nose, mouth, chin,
With white teeth inside my mouth.
Hand, other hand, one, two,
Foot, other foot, one, two,
Head, nose, mouth, chin,
With white teeth inside my mouth.

For more about Lámh, lámh eile, go to:
http://www.mamalisa.com/?t=es&p=3473.

There, you'll find a video performance.

Little Jennie Whiteface
(Riddle)

Little Jennie Whiteface
Has a red nose,
The longer she lives
The shorter she grows.

Notes

*This is the Irish version of the riddle **Little Nancy Etticoat** (http://www.mamalisa.com/?t=hes&p=1636&l=L).*

Photos & Illustrations

Comments

Scroll down for the answer to the riddle - though for this one you have a great hint!
*
*
*
*
*
*
*
*
*
*
*
Answer: A lit candle.

For more about Little Jennie Whiteface, go to:
http://www.mamalisa.com/?t=es&p=2960.

May the Road Rise to Meet You
(Irish Blessing)

May the road rise up to meet you.
May the wind be always at your back.
May the sun shine warm upon your face;
The rains fall soft upon your fields
And until we meet again,
May God hold you
In the hollow of his hand.

Notes

Here's another version that's used as an Irish toast:

May the road rise to meet you.
May the wind be always at your back
May you be in heaven half an hour
Before the Devil knows you're dead.

For more about May the Road Rise to Meet You, go to:
http://www.mamalisa.com/?t=es&p=3025.

There, you'll find an MP3 tune and a video performance.

35

Me Mother Is Gone to Church
(Kids' Chant)

Ahem! Ahem!
Me mother is gone to church.
She told me not to play with you
Because you're in the dirt.
It isn't because you're dirty,
It isn't because you're clean,
It's because you have the whoopin' cough
And eat margarine!

Comments

John wrote, "Heard this at a Clancy Bros. concert about a million years ago."

For more about Me Mother Is Gone to Church, go to:
http://www.mamalisa.com/?t=es&p=422.

Michael Finnigan
(Children's Song)

There was a boy called Michael Finnigan,
He grew whiskers on his chin-igan.
The wind came out and blew them in again.
Poor old Michael Finnigan, begin again.

There was an old man named Michael Finnigan,
Who went off fishing with a pinnigan.
He caught a fish, but it fell in again.
Poor old Michael Finnigan.

There was an old man named Michael Finnigan,
Who caught a cold and couldn't get well again.
Then he died, and had to begin again.
Poor old Michael Finnigan.

Comments

There are many different versions to this song. Katherine contributed the 1st verse above. The other two verses appear the most often in other variations of "Michael Finnigan".

For more about Michael Finnigan, go to:
http://www.mamalisa.com/?t=es&p=420.

There, you'll find sheet music and a MIDI melody.

Mitty Matty Had a Hen

Mitty Matty Had a Hen
(Nursery Rhyme)

Mitty Matty had a hen
She laid eggs for gentlemen
Sometimes nine and sometimes ten
Mitty matty's fine fat hen!

Notes

Here's another version from Ireland from "The Counting-out Rhymes of Children" (1888) by Henry Carrington Bolton:

Mitty Matty had a hen,
She lays white eggs for gentlemen.
Gentlemen come every day,

Mitty Matty runs away.
Hi! ho! who is at home?
Father, mother, Jumping Joan.
O-U-T out,
Take off the latch and walk out.

For more about Mitty Matty Had a Hen, go to:
http://www.mamalisa.com/?t=es&p=3507.

Oíche Shamhna (Halloween, Halloween)

*This is an Irish Gaelic version of **Frère Jacques**
(http://mamalisa.com/?t=es&p=180&c=22) that's about Halloween. The song
mentions Barmbrack, which is an Irish yeast bread that's served for the holiday.
It's often cooked with a toy ring in it and the person who gets the ring is supposed
to be the one who will get married within the year.*

Oíche Shamhna
(Irish Gaelic Halloween Song)

Oíche Shamhna, Oíche Shamhna,
Báirín, breac, báirín breac,
Úlla is cnónna, úlla is cnónna,
Is maith liom iad, is maith liom iad.

Halloween, Halloween
(English Translation)

Halloween, Halloween,
Barmbrack, barmbrack,
Apples and nuts, apples and nuts,
I like them, I like them.

For more about Oíche Shamhna , go to:
http://www.mamalisa.com/?t=es&p=3492.

There, you'll find a video performance.

Old Dan Tucker
(Nursery Rhyme)

Old Dan Tucker was a fine old man
Washed his face in a frying pan
Combed his hair with a wagon wheel
And died with a toothache in his heel.

So get out the way for Old Dan Tucker
He's too late to get his supper
Supper is over and breakfast's cookin'
Old Dan Tucker just stands there lookin'.

For more about Old Dan Tucker, go to:
http://www.mamalisa.com/?t=es&p=3535.

There, you'll find a video performance.

Old Mother Witch

This can also be recited as "Old Nanny Witch".

Old Mother Witch
(Nursery Rhyme)

Old Mother Witch,
She fell in a ditch,
She picked up a penny,
And thought she was rich.

For more about Old Mother Witch, go to:
http://www.mamalisa.com/?t=es&p=3543.

Old Riley's Daughter

Here's a kids-friendly version of a more bawdy Irish song that's thought to date back to the 18th century....

Old Riley's Daughter
(Traditional Song)

As I was sittin' by the fire
Thinking of old Riley's daughter,
Suddenly a thought come into my mind
I'd like to marry old Riley's daughter.

(Chorus)
Giddy-I-ay, giddy-I-ay, giddy-I-ay
To the one-eyed Riley,
Giddy-I-ay, (ACTION: KNOCK, KNOCK, KNOCK)
Play it on your old bass drum.

Riley played on a big bass drum
Riley had a mind for murder and slaughter
Riley had a bright, red, glittering eye,
He kept that eye on his lovely daughter.

(Chorus)

Her hair was black and her eyes were blue,
The colonel and the major and the captain sought her,
The sergeant and the private and the drummer boy too
Never had a chance with Riley's daughter.

(Chorus)

I got me a ring and a parson too
I got me a scratch in the married quarter,
Settled me down to the peaceful life
Happy as a king with Riley's daughter.

(Chorus)

Suddenly a footstep on the stairs,
Who should it be but Riley up for slaughter
With two pistols in his hands
Looking for the man who had married his daughter.

(Chorus)

I grabbed old Riley by the hair
Rammed his head in a pail of water,
Fired his pistols into the air
A darn sight quicker than I married his daughter.

(Chorus)

For more about Old Riley's Daughter, go to:
http://www.mamalisa.com/?t=es&p=3467.

There, you'll find a video performance.

One Potato, Two Potato

Although ONE POTATO, TWO POTATO *is recited all over the English speaking world, it's especially loved in Ireland given the importance of potatoes in Irish cuisine.*

One Potato, Two Potato
(Counting-out Rhyme)

One potato, two potato,
Three potato, four,
Five potato, six potato,
Seven potato, more!

Game Instructions

All of the kids put our their two fists. One kid goes around tapping the other kids' fists with his fist. The one whose fist he ends the rhyme on is out (that kid puts that fist behind his back). Then go around again and again until only one fist is left. The one that is left at the end of all the rounds is "It".

For more about One Potato, Two Potato, go to:
http://www.mamalisa.com/?t=es&p=3536.

There, you'll find an MP3 tune and a video performance.

43

Onery, Twoery, Dickery, Davey
(Counting-out Rhyme)

Onery, twoery, dickery, Davey
Horrible, crackable, ninery, Lavey
Discontented American time
Humbledy, bumbledy, number nine.

For more about Onery, Twoery, Dickery, Davey, go to:
http://www.mamalisa.com/?t=es&p=2933.

One, Two, Three O'Leary
(Ball Bouncing Song)

One, two, three O'Leary
Four, five, six O'Leary
Seven, eight, nine O'Leary
Ten O'Leary caught it.*

Notes

Alternate line, "Ten O'Leary, Postman!"

Game Instructions

Bounce the ball on each number. Every time you say "O'Leary" pass your leg over the ball. Then catch the ball on the last line.

For more about One, Two, Three O'Leary , go to:
http://www.mamalisa.com/?t=es&p=3481.

Paddy on the Railway
(Nursery Rhyme)

Paddy on the railway
Picking up stones,
Along came an engine
And broke Paddy's bones.

"Oh!" said Paddy,
"That's not fair."
"Oh!" said the engine driver,
"I don't care."

For more about Paddy on the Railway, go to:
http://www.mamalisa.com/?t=es&p=3515.

There, you'll find a video performance.

Postman

Postman
(Jump Rope Rhyme)

Early in the morning at 6 o'clock
I can hear the postman knock,
Postman, postman drop your letter,
Postman, postman pick it up.

For more about Postman, go to: **http://www.mamalisa.com/?t=es&p=3518**.

Sally Go Round the Moon

Sally Go Round the Moon
(Children's Song)

Sally go round the moon
Sally go round the stars
Sally go round the moon
On a Sunday afternoon, whoops!

Sally go round the moon
Sally go round the stars
Sally go round the moon
On a Sunday afternoon, whoops!

Sally go round the moon...

Notes

You can repeat this as long as you'd like!

Game Instructions

Kids go around in a circle and on "whoops" either change direction they're going around or jump and then repeat the verse.

For more about Sally Go Round the Moon, go to:
http://www.mamalisa.com/?t=es&p=3510.

Seoithín, Seo Hó (Hush-a-bye, Baby)

SEOITHÍN, SEO HÓ *is an old Irish Gaelic lullaby. Some people in the olden days believed that fairies would abduct babies. That's why there's the threat in this song that the baby must go to sleep before the fairies can lure him away.*

Humming is often weaved between the verses in Irish lullabies.

Seoithín, Seo Hó
(Irish Gaelic Lullaby)

Seoithín, seo hó, mo stór é, mo leanbh
Mo sheoid gan cealg, mo chuid gan tsaoil mhór
Seothín seo ho, nach mór é an taitneamh
Mo stóirín na leaba, na chodladh gan brón.

Curfá:
A leanbh mo chléibh go n-eirí do chodhladh leat
Séan is sonas gach oíche do chóir

Tá mise le do thaobh ag guídhe ort na mbeannacht
Seothín a leanbh is codail go foill.

Ar mhullach an tí tá síodha geala
Faol chaoin re an Earra ag imirt is spoirt
Seo iad aniar iad le glaoch ar mo leanbh
Le mian é tharraingt isteach san lios mór.

Curfá

Hush-a-bye, Baby
(English Translation)

Hush-a-bye, baby, my darling, my child
My flawless jewel, my piece of the world
Hush-a-bye, baby, isn't it a great joy
My little one in bed without any sorrows.

(Chorus)
Child of my heart, sleep calmly
And well all night and be happy
I'm by your side praying for blessings on you,
Hush-a-bye, baby and sleep for now.

On top of the house there are white fairies
Playing and frolicking under the gentle moonlight
Here they come calling my baby
To draw him into their great fairy mound.

(Chorus)

Comments

You can hear a recording of another version of **Seoithín, seo hó** *here*
(http://www.joeheaney.org/default.asp?contentID=1032). In that version, which is
sung by Joe Éinniú (Heaney), he talks about the song and how humming was
weaved into it. He said, "I remember my grandmother singing this for my youngest
sister, and she used to hum…after she sang the verse, she used to hum, too."

For more about Seoithín, Seo Hó, go to:
http://www.mamalisa.com/?t=es&p=3482.

There, you'll find a video performance.

Shule Aroon

This song is believed to be from the 17th century or early 18th century. It's about a woman whose love has enlisted in the brigade to find his fortune...

Shule Aroon
(Ballad)

I would I were on yonder hill,
'Tis there I'd sit and cry my fill,
And every tear would turn a mill.

(Chorus in Irish Gaelic)*
Is go d-teidh tu, a mhurnin, slan !
Siubhail, siubhail, siubhail, a ruin !
Siubhail go socair, agus siubhail go ciuin,
Siubhail go d-ti an doras agus eulaigh liom,
Is go d-teidh tu, a mhurnin, slan !

I'll sell my rock, I'll sell my reel,
I'll sell my only spinning-wheel,
To buy for my love a sword of steel**.

(Chorus in Irish Gaelic)

I'll dye my petticoats, I'll dye them red,
And round the world I'll beg my bread,

Until my parents shall wish me dead.

(Chorus in Irish Gaelic)

I wish, I wish, I wish in vain,
I wish I had my heart again,
And vainly think I'd not complain.

(Chorus in Irish Gaelic)

But now my love has gone to France,
To try his fortune to advance ;
If he e'er come back, 'tis but a chance.

(Chorus in Irish Gaelic)

Notes

Chorus Translation and Pronunciation:

APPROXIMATE PRONUNCIATION OF THE CHORUS:

Iss go dee too, a vourneen slaun.
Shoo-il, shoo-il, shoo-il, a rooin,
Shoo-il go socair, oggus shoo-il go kioon,
Shoo-il go dee an doras, oggus euli liom,
Iss go dee too, a vourneen slaun.

Literal Translation:

And mayst thou go, O darling, safe.
Move, move, move, O treasure !
Move quietly, and move gently,
Move to the door, and elope with me,
And mayst thou go, O darling, safe.

Versified Translation:

And safe for aye may my darling be !
Come, come, come, O love !
Quietly come to me, softly move,
Come to the door, and away we'll flee,
And safe for aye may my darling be !

Chorus translated by Dr. Sigerson for IRISH MINSTRELSY *(1888), edited by H. Halliday Sparling.*

**This is a grand gesture, for the woman is proposing to sell all of her spinning supplies, which would have sustained her by supplying her with thread, to buy her love a sword, i.e. to protect him.

"Rock", "reel", and "spinning-wheel" are all related to spinning. Spinning is the

process of making thread, usually to later make material on a loom.

The "rock" is also called the distaff. The distaff was a long stick that held the prepared fibers of material for making the thread. It was attached to the spinning wheel. The "reel" is where the thread would go after it was spun. (It would wind around the reel.)

Photos & Illustrations

For more about Shule Aroon, go to: **http://www.mamalisa.com/?t=es&p=2159**.

There, you'll find sheet music, a MIDI melody and a video performance.

Skinny Malink

In order to fully appreciate this rhyme, you need to know that a "skinny malink" is someone who's very skinny and a "melodeon" is a type of accordion.

Skinny Malink
(Rhyme)

Skinny malink
Melodeon legs,
Big banana feet,
Went to the doctors
And couldn't get a seat.
When he got a seat,
He fell fast asleep
Skinny malink
Melodeon legs,
Big banana feet.

For more about Skinny Malink, go to:
http://www.mamalisa.com/?t=es&p=3532.

So Early in the Morning
(Children's Song)

When I was young, I had no sense,
I bought a fiddle for eighteen pence,
The only tune that I could play
Was "Over the Hills and Far Away".

(Chorus)
So early in the morning,
So early in the morning,
So early in the morning,
Before the break of day.

My Aunt Jane she called me in
She gave me tea out of a tin,
Half a bag of sugar on the top
And three black lumps out of her wee shop.

(Chorus)

For more about So Early in the Morning, go to:
http://www.mamalisa.com/?t=es&p=3489.

There, you'll find a video performance.

Tá Mé 'mo Shuí (I am Up)

Tá Mé 'mo Shuí
(Irish Gaelic Ballad)

Tá mé mo shuí ó d`éirigh`n ghealach aréir
Ag cur teine síos gan scíth is á fadó go géar
Tá bunadh a` tí `na luí is tá mise liom féin
Tá na coiligh ag glaoch `san saol `na gcodladh ach mé.

Sheacht mh`anam déag do bhéal do mhala is do ghrua
Do shúil ghorm ghlé-gheal fár thréig mé aiteas is suairc
Le cumha do dhiaidh ní léir dom an bealach a shiúil
Is a charaid mo chléibh tá na sléibhte `dul idir mé`s tú

Deiridh lucht léinn gur claoite an galar an grá
Char admhaigh mé é is é `ndiaidh mo chroí istigh a chrá
Aicid róghéar faraor nár sheachain mé í
Chuir sí arraing is céad go géar trí cheart-lár mo chroí.

Casadh bean-tsí dom thíos ag Lios Bhéal an Átha
D`fhiafraigh mé di an scaoilfeadh glas ar bith grá
Is é dúirt sí os íseal i mbriathra soineannta sáimh
"Nuair a théann sé fán chroí cha scaoiltear as é go bráth."

I am Up
(English Translation)

I am up since the moon arose last night
Building a fire over and over again and keeping it lit
The family is in bed and here I am alone,
The cocks are crowing and the whole country is asleep, all but me.

I love your mouth, your eyebrows and your cheeks,
Your bright blue eyes for which I gave up contentment
in longing for you, I cannot see the road to walk,
Friend of my bosom, the mountains are between you and me.

Scholars say that love is a disease,
I've never admitted it before now that my heart is broken,
It's a painful disease that unfortunately I haven't avoided.
It's sending a hundred arrows through the core of my heart.

I met a fairy women at the hollow of Béal an Átha
I asked her to banish any love that I have

She said in words very quietly and simply,
"When love goes to the heart it is never banished."

For more about Tá Mé 'mo Shuí, go to:
http://www.mamalisa.com/?t=es&p=3486.

There, you'll find a video performance.

The Beggarman
(Traditional Song)

I am a little beggarman, a begging I have been
For three score or more in this little isle of green
I'm known along the Liffey down to Segue
I'm known by the the the name of Johnny Dhu.

Of all the trades a-going, the begging is the best
For when a man is tired he can sit down and rest
He can beg for his dinner, he has nothing else to do
Only cut around the corner with his old rigadoo*.

I slept in a barn way down in Currabawn
A wet night it was, but I slept until the dawn
There was holes in the roof and the raindrops coming thru
When the rats and the cats they were playing peek-a-boo.

Who should awaken but the woman of the house
With her white spotted apron and her calico blouse
She began to frighten and I said, "Boo!
Well, don't be afraid, it's only Johnny Dhu."

I met a little flaxy-haired girl one day
"Good morrow little flaxy-haired girl," I did say.
"Good morrow little beggarman and how do you do
With your rags and your tags and your auld rigadoo."

I'll buy a pair of leggins and a collar and a tie
And a nice young lady I'll fetch by and by
I'll buy a pair of goggles and color them blue**
And an old-fashioned lady I will make her too.

Over the road with my pack upon my back
Over the fields with my great heavy sack
With holes in my shoes and my toes a peeping thru
Singing, skin-a-ma-rink-a-doodle with my auld rigadoo.

I must be going to bed for it's getting late at night
The fire is all raked and out goes light
So now you've heard the story of my auld rigadoo
So good night and God be with you, from auld Johnny Dhu.

Notes

*A rigadoo is a type of dance and also a walking stick.
**This line was originally, "We'll buy ya a pair of leggings and color them blue"
which could mean that they'd color them blue to signify she's married.

For more about The Beggarman, go to:
http://www.mamalisa.com/?t=es&p=3505.

There, you'll find a video performance.

The Fairy Nurse

This lullaby is thought to be from an old Gaelic Irish lullaby that's been translated into English by Edward Walsh. Some sources say it was originally written in English by Walsh but that the tune is from ancient Ireland. We haven't been able to find a Gaelic version.

This lullaby is about a baby who was stolen by the fairies...

The Fairy Nurse
(Lullaby)

Sweet babe! a golden cradle holds thee,
And soft the snow-white fleece enfolds thee;
In airy bower I'll watch thy sleeping,
Where branchy trees to the breeze are sweeping.
Shuheen, sho, lulo lo!

When mothers languish broken-hearted,
When young wives are from husbands parted,
Ah! little think the keeners (1) lonely,
They weep some time-worn fairy only.
Shuheen sho, lulo lo!

Within our magic halls of brightness,
Trips many a foot of snowy whiteness;
Stolen maidens, queens of fairy-
And kings and chiefs a sluagh shee (2) airy.
Shuheen sho, lulo lo!

Rest thee, babe ! I love thee dearly,
And as thy mortal mother nearly;
Ours is the swiftest steed and proudest.
That moves where the tramp of the host is loudest.
Shuheen sho, lulo lo!

Rest thee, babe! for soon thy slumbers
Shall flee at the magic koelshie's (3) numbers;
In airy bower I'll watch thy sleeping,
Where branchy trees to the breeze are sweeping.
Shuheen sho, lulo lo!

Notes

(1) Keeners - mourners - people wailing and lamenting the dead
(2) Fairy Host
(3) Fairy Music

Below is a shorter, less ominous version of this lullaby.

Sweet babe, a golden cradle holds thee,
Shuheen sho, lulo lo!
And soft the snow-white fleece enfolds thee,
Shuheen sho, lulo lo!
In airy bower I'll watch thy sleeping,
Shuheen sho, lulo lo!
Where branchy trees to the breeze are sweeping,
Shuheen sho, lulo lo!

For more about The Fairy Nurse, go to:
http://www.mamalisa.com/?t=es&p=3497.

The Lambs on the Green Hills

There are many versions of this song. It's sad, but pretty.

The Lambs on the Green Hills
(Traditional Song)

The lambs on the green hills, they sport and they play
And many strawberries grow round the salt sea,
How sad is my heart when my love is away
How many's the ships sails the ocean.

The bride and bride's party to church they did go,
The bride she rode foremost, she bears the best show,
But I followed after with my heart filled with woe
To see my love wed to another.

The first place I saw her was in the church stand
Gold rings on her fingers and her love by the hand,
Says I, ma wee lassie, I will be the man
Although you are wed to another.

The next place I saw her was on the way home,
I ran on before her, not knowing where to roam.
Says I, ma wee lassie, I'll be by your side
Although you are wed to another.

Stop, stop, says the groomsman, til I speak a word
Will you venture your life on the point of my sword,
For courtin' so slowly you've lost this fair maid
So, be gone for you'll never enjoy her.

O make now my grave, both large, wide and deep
And sprinkle it over with flowers so sweet,
And lay me down in it to take my last sleep,
For that's the best way to forget her.

For more about The Lambs on the Green Hills, go to:
http://www.mamalisa.com/?t=es&p=3438.

There, you'll find a video performance.

The Parting Glass

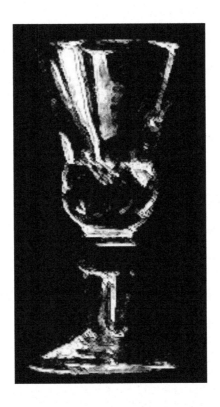

The Parting Glass is sometimes sung when friends part.

The Parting Glass
(Traditional Farewell Song)

Of all the money e'er I had,
I spent it in good company.
And all the harm I've ever done,
Alas! it was to none but me.
And all I've done for want of wit
To mem'ry now I can't recall
So fill to me the parting glass
Good night and joy be with you all.

Oh, all the comrades e'er I had,
They're sorry for my going away,

And all the sweethearts e'er I had,
They'd wish me one more day to stay,
But since it falls unto my lot,
That I should rise and you should not,
I'll gently rise and softly call,
Good night and joy be with you all.

If I had money enough to spend,
And leisure time to sit awhile,
There is a fair maid in this town,
That sorely has my heart beguiled.
Her rosy cheeks and ruby lips,
I own she has my heart in thrall,
Then fill to me the parting glass,
Good night and joy be with you all.

Notes

There's a Scottish version of this song too, an early version of which appeared in print in the 1770's. According to Wikipedia, "The song is doubtless older than its 1770 appearance in broadside, as it was recorded in the Skene Manuscript, a collection of Scottish airs written at various dates between 1615 and 1635. It was known at least as early as 1605, when a portion of the first stanza was written in a farewell letter, as a poem now known as 'Armstrong's Goodnight', by one of the Border Reivers [raiders along the Anglo-Scottish border] executed that year for the murder in 1600 of Sir John Carmichael, Warden of the Scottish West March."

Here's "Armstrong's Goodnight":

*This night is my departing night,
For here nae langer must I stay;
There's neither friend nor foe o' mine,
But wishes me away.*

*What I have done thro' lack of wit,
I never, never can recall;
I hope ye're a' my friends as yet;
Good night and joy be with you all.*

For more about The Parting Glass, go to:
http://www.mamalisa.com/?t=es&p=3524.

There, you'll find a video performance.

There Once Were Two Cats of Kilkenny
(Nursery Rhyme)

There once were two cats of Kilkenny,
Each thought there was one cat too many,
So they fought and they fit,
And they scratched and they bit,
Till, excepting their nails
And the tips of their tails,
Instead of two cats, there weren't any.

For more about There Once Were Two Cats of Kilkenny, go to:
http://www.mamalisa.com/?t=es&p=1390.

There, you'll find a video performance.

There Was a Little Man and He Had a Little Gun

"I live in Ireland, and my grandad used to sing it to me like this..." -Sarah

There Was a Little Man and He Had a Little Gun
(Children's Song)

There was a little man and he had a little gun
And up the chimney he did run
With a belly full of fat and an old tall hat
And a pancake stuck to his bum bum bum.

Notes

Sarah wrote, "I'm only 19, so it wasn't very long ago that my grandad sang it to me. He used to sing it to my dad as well when he was little. I'm guessing it's been passed down through the generations."

For more about There Was a Little Man and He Had a Little Gun, go to:
http://www.mamalisa.com/?t=es&p=3404.

The Worms Crawl In (An Irish Version)

"These are the words we sang at our Scout Meetings in Ireland..." -Jacqueline

The Worms Crawl In (An Irish Version)
(Traditional Song)

The worms crawl in,
The worms crawl out,
They crawl in thin and
They crawl out stout,
Yo Ho Yo Ho
How happy we will be.

For more about The Worms Crawl In (An Irish Version), go to:
http://www.mamalisa.com/?t=es&p=3399.

Three Gray Geese

Three Gray Geese
(Nursery Rhyme)

Three gray geese
In a green field grazing,
Gray were the geese
And green was the grazing.

For more about Three Gray Geese, go to:
http://www.mamalisa.com/?t=es&p=3511.

Too Ra Loo Ra Loo Ral (That's an Irish Lullaby)
(Traditional Song)

Over in Killarney,
Many years ago,
Me mither sang a song to me
In tones so sweet and low.
Just a simple little ditty,
In her good ould Irish way,
And I'd give the world if she could sing
That song to me this day.

Too-ra-loo-ra-loo-ral,
Too-ra-loo-ra-li,
Too-ra-loo-ra-loo-ral,
Hush, now don't you cry!
Too-ra-loo-ra-loo-ral,
Too-ra-loo-ra-li,
Too-ra-loo-ra-loo-ral,
That's an Irish lullaby.

Oft, in dreams I wander
To that cot again,
I feel her arms a huggin' me
As when she held me then.
And I hear her voice a hummin'
To me as in days of yore,
When she used to rock me fast asleep
Outside the cabin door.

Too-ra-loo-ra-loo-ral,
Too-ra-loo-ra-li,
Too-ra-loo-ra-loo-ral,
Hush, now don't you cry!
Too-ra-loo-ra-loo-ral,
Too-ra-loo-ra-li,
Too-ra-loo-ra-loo-ral,
That's an Irish lullaby.

Notes

This song was written by James Royce Shannon in 1913.

For more about Too Ra Loo Ra Loo Ral
(That's an Irish Lullaby), go to: **http://www.mamalisa.com/?t=es&p=421**.

There, you'll find a MIDI melody and a video performance.

Two Little Dickie Birds
(Nursery Rhyme)

Two little dickie birds,
Sitting on a wall;
One named Peter,
One named Paul.
Fly away Peter!
Fly away Paul!
Come Back Peter!
Come Back Paul!

For more about Two Little Dickie Birds, go to:
http://www.mamalisa.com/?t=es&p=3464.

Wall Flowers

Wallflowers are wildflowers in Ireland.

Wall Flowers
(Circle Game Song)

Wallflowers, wallflowers,
Growing up so high,
We're pretty mermaids
And we shall not die.

Except for (girl's name),
She's the only one.
Turn her around, turn her around
So she cannot face the sun.

Notes

Here's another version:

Wall flowers, wall flowers,
Growing up so high,
He had the measles
He'll never ever die.

*****

Here's another version as submitted by Miss H. E. Harvey of Howth, Dublin to
"The Traditional Games of England, Scotland, and Ireland" (1898) edited by Alice
Bertha Gomme:

Wall-flowers, wall-flowers,
Growin' up so high,
Neither me nor my baby
Shall ever wish to die,
Especially [girl's name],
she's the prettiest flower.
She can dance, and she can sing,
and she can tell the hour,
With her wee-waw, wy-waw,
Turn her face to the wall.
(OR "Turn your back to all the game.")

Game Instructions

The children form a ring by joining hands. They all dance slowly round, singing
the words. When the one child is named by the ring she turns round, so that her
face is turned to the outside of the ring and her back inside. She still clasps hands
with those on either side of her, and dances or walks round with them. This is
continued until all the players have turned and are facing outwards.

Photos & Illustrations

For more about Wall Flowers , go to: **http://www.mamalisa.com/?t=es&p=3460**.

Wee Weaver

Wee Weaver
(Traditional Song)

I am a wee weaver confined to my loom,
And my love she is fairer than the red rose in June.
She's loved by all young men and that does grieve me,
There's a heart in my bosom for lovely Mary.

As Willie and Mary rode by yon shady bower,
Where Willie and Mary spent many a happy hour.
Where the blackbirds and thrushes do concert and chorus,
The praises of Mary and love fair and sure.

As Willie and Mary rode by yon river side,
Said Willie to Mary: "Will you be my bride?"
This couple got married and they roam no more,
They have pleasures and treasures and love fair and sure.

For more about Wee Weaver, go to: **http://www.mamalisa.com/?t=es&p=3474**.

There, you'll find a video performance.

65

When Irish Eyes Are Smiling
(Traditional Song)

(Chorus)
When Irish eyes are smiling, sure 'tis like a morn in spring.
In the lilt of Irish laughter you can hear the angels sing,
When Irish hearts are happy all the world seems bright and gay,
And when Irish eyes are smiling, sure, they steal your heart away.

There's a tear in your eye and I'm wondering why,
For it never should be there at all.
With such power in your smile, sure a stone you'd beguile,
And there's never a teardrop should fall,
When your sweet lilting laughter's like some fairy song
And your eyes sparkle bright as can be.
You should laugh all the while and all other times smile,
So now smile a smile for me.

(Chorus)

For your smile is a part of the love in your heart,
And it makes even sunshine more bright.
Like the linnet's sweet song, crooning all the day long.
Comes your laughter so tender and light.
For the springtime of life is the best time of all,
With never a pain or regret.
While the springtime is ours, thru all of life's hours,
Let us smile each chance we get.

(Chorus)

Notes

*Written in 1912 by Irish American Chauncey Olcott and also George Graff, Jr.,
music composed by Ernest Ball. It was written in tribute to Ireland.*

For more about When Irish Eyes Are Smiling, go to:
http://www.mamalisa.com/?t=es&p=3439.

There, you'll find a video performance.

Thanks and Acknowledgements!

We're so grateful to everyone who helped us gather the material for this book!

Go raibh maith agaibh!

4 Are You a Witch or Are You a Fairy?
Original image from "More English Fairy Tales", illustrated by John D. Batten and heavily graphically edited by Mama Lisa.

5 As I Went up the Apple Tree
The illustration comes from "Little Wide-awake, Annual for Children" (1883) by Lucy D Sale Barker - it was graphically altered by Mama Lisa.

7 Bog Down in The Valley-O
Many thanks to Nyango M. Nambangi of the **Minnesota African Women's Association** (http://www.mawanet.org/) for contributing this song.

Images from "Bog-trotting for Orchids" (1904) by Grace Greylock Niles - graphically edited by Mama Lisa.

9 Briney Ole Lynn
Many thanks to Marcy Miller for contributing this song.

10 Bryan O'Lynn
A slightly longer (and racier) version of this song can be found in "**The Emerald; or, Book of Irish melodies** (http://www.archive.org/details/emeraldorbookofi00newy)" (1863).

11 Cockles and Mussels
Many thanks to Katherine Quinn for contributing this song.

Thanks also to Margaret B. for contributing the second version of this song and for sharing her lovely YouTube video rendition of MOLLY MALONE. We've posted another YouTube video by Margaret called *Spider's Web* (HTTP://MAMALISA.COM/?T=ES&P=1213&C=23). You can click the link for the lyrics and video. You can see **other YouTube videos by Margaret** (http://www.youtube.com/user/QueenMAB418) on her YouTube Home Page.

Illustration compiled by Mama Lisa.

13 Connemara Cradle Song
1st Photo from Connemara is from **Wikipedia**
(http://en.wikipedia.org/wiki/File:Twelve_pins.JPG).

2nd photo of a currach is also from **Wikipedia**
(http://en.wikipedia.org/wiki/File:FloatingCurraghBedford.JPG). It's a
reconstruction of a British Curragh from the 1st century that's made of wicker
work and covered with 3 cow hides."

17 Do You Love an Apple?
Original image comes from "Apple Growing in California" (1914) - it was heavily
edited by Mama Lisa.

18 Fairy Lullaby
"The English version is by Mr. Sigerson, who has preserved the rhythm of the
original, in a faithful translation." -Shamrock (Vol. 8 - 1870)

Image from an old fairy book - heavily edited by Mama Lisa.

19 Four Ducks on a Pond
Image from "The Baby's Bouquet" by Walter Crane - graphically edited by Mama
Lisa.

21 Goodie on a Saucer
The image comes from an ad for Junket that was in "American Cookery", Volume
24 (1920) and it was graphically edited by Mama Lisa.

22 Head of Hair Forehead Bare
Thanks to Caroline for sharing her version of this rhyme.

23 Hiddledy, Diddledy, Dumpty
From L. M. in Limerick, Ireland as found in "The Counting-out Rhymes of
Children" (1888) by Henry Carrington Bolton.

27 I'm a Tiny Tiny Thing
I found this rhyme when looking up "ring-a-ring" in the Oxford English Dictionary
while researching the rhyme, "**Ring-a-ring O' Roses**
(http://www.mamalisa.com/?t=hes&p=1456&l=R)".

29 I See the Moon, The Moon Sees Me
This can be found in "English as We Speak it in Ireland" (1910) by P. W. Joyce.
The 1st illustration is a compilation by Mama Lisa from old book images.

33 Little Jennie Whiteface
This rhyme can be found in "English As We Speak It in Ireland" (1910) by P. W. Joyce. The illustration is from MOTHER GOOSE, THE ORIGINAL VOLLAND EDITION (1915), edited and arranged by Eulalie Osgood Grover and illustrated by Frederick Richardson (with some graphical editing by Mama Lisa).

35 Me Mother Is Gone to Church
Many thanks to John G. May for contributing this song.

36 Michael Finnigan
Many thanks to Katherine Quinn for contributing this song. Katherine wrote, "My grandma always used to sing 'Michael Finnigan' to me, except she used to sing 'Michael Quinnigan', as my brother's name is Michael Quinn."

37 Mitty Matty Had a Hen
The illustration comes from "The Lullaby : With Original Engravings" (c1851). It was graphically edited by Mama Lisa.

43 Onery, Twoery, Dickery, Davey
Many thanks to Barbara Vaughan for sharing her grandfather's version of Onery, Twoery.

46 Postman
Illustration from "Month by Month Books" (1904) and edited by Mama Lisa.

47 Sally Go Round the Moon
Image composed by Mama Lisa by graphically editing 2 different pictures from very old nursery rhyme books.

48 Seoithín, Seo Hó (Hush-a-bye, Baby)
The illustration comes from "The Lullaby : with original engravings" (c1851). It was graphically edited by Mama Lisa.

49 Shule Aroon
This song can be found in: IRISH MINSTRELSY (1888) by H. Halliday Sparling, THE POEM-BOOK OF THE GAEL edited by Eleanor Hull (1912), THE SONG LORE OF IRELAND ERIN'S STORY IN MUSIC AND VERSE by Redfern Mason and THE GOLDEN TREASURY OF IRISH SONGS AND LYRICS by Charles Welsh (1907).

Many thanks to Monique Palomares for the midi tune.

The 1st illustration is from BANBURY CHAP BOOKS, and the 2nd illustration is from THE TALE OF THE SPINNING-WHEEL (1903), illustrated by Emily Vanderpoel.

54 The Fairy Nurse
Translated from the original Irish Gaelic by Edward Walsh or originally written in English by Edward Walsh.

56 The Parting Glass
Image from "Collecting Old Glass, English and Irish" (1918) by Sir James Henry Yoxall, graphically edited by Mama Lisa.

58 There Was a Little Man and He Had a Little Gun
Many thanks to Sarah for sharing this rhyme!

59 The Worms Crawl In (An Irish Version)
Many thanks to Jacqueline Lewis Leary for contributing this song.

61 Too Ra Loo Ra Loo Ral (That's an Irish Lullaby)
Many thanks to Melissa for contributing this song. Her mom used to sing it to her when she was a little girl. Thanks also to Eduardo de Lima Pereira for helping us with the tune and to Monique Palomares for creating the midi music.

63 Wall Flowers
Photo from **Wikipedia** (http://en.wikipedia.org/wiki/Erysimum_cheiri). Diagram of how to play the game comes from "The Traditional Games of England, Scotland, and Ireland" (1898) edited by Alice Bertha Gomme.

64 Wee Weaver
Image comes from "Cotton and Linen" (1922) by Eliza Bailey Thompson.

About Mama Lisa's World

Mama Lisa's World (**www.mamalisa.com**) is the internet's premier destination for children's songs from around the globe and for discussions of international culture. It features thousands of traditional songs from over a hundred countries and cultures and a major collection of Mother Goose Rhymes. Mama Lisa's Blog focuses on global recipes, holiday traditions, poetry and lively conversations about childhood around the world.

About the Staff

Lisa Yannucci (Mama Lisa)
Lisa was inspired to start Mama Lisa's World in the mid 1990's, when her young son first became interested in nursery rhymes. She recorded several Mother Goose songs onto a computer and programmed them to play when he clicked a picture. He loved it and she became fascinated with the power of the internet to enrich the lives of children. She made the site public and has since used her background in languages and culture, and her talent as an illustrator, to oversee its tremendous growth.

Jason Pomerantz
Jason (Lisa's husband) has worked in magazine, book and web publishing for over twenty years. His personal projects have included several websites and podcasts. Along with his editorial contributions, he oversees the business and technical aspects of Mama Lisa's World.

Monique Palomares
Monique grew up at the crossroads of three cultures in the Occitan region of France. She is fluent in French, Spanish, English and Occitan and has a working knowledge of many other languages including Italian. Her years as a first grade teacher and her love of children and linguistics give her a unique insight into the power of music and song all over the world.

About You

Mama Lisa's World is made up of contributions from ordinary people from all over the globe. Please visit us at **www.mamalisa.com** and say hello! We want to hear about your childhood memories, your favorite recipes, your holidays and anything else you'd like to share about your culture.

Thank you for being part of our community!

Made in the USA
Middletown, DE
09 September 2021